TO ALL THE
KIDS IN THE
WORLD
DREAM BIG..
BELIEVE IN
YOURSELF
AND NEVER
GIVE UP.WE
BELIEVE IN
YOU

# TABLE OF CONTENT

# Fun coloring ideas with sneakers

The Solar System

M
V
E
M
J
S
U
N
The Solar System

Aunty
TABITHA
Brown

# MRS. TABITHA BROWN

wife

Aunty

ENCOURAGES

GOD IS LOVE
DAUGHTER
SPEAKER
AND SHE DOES SO MUCH MORE
ACTOR
AUTHOR
BUISNESS OWNER
SOCIAL MEDIA INFLUENCER

## SHE DOES IT ALL
## IN HER SNEAKERS

HAVE FUN AND CREATE ANYTHING

SONIC KIDS IDEA

NIKE

BE CREATIVE

The Solar System
The Solar System

# CREATED BY TODDLERS

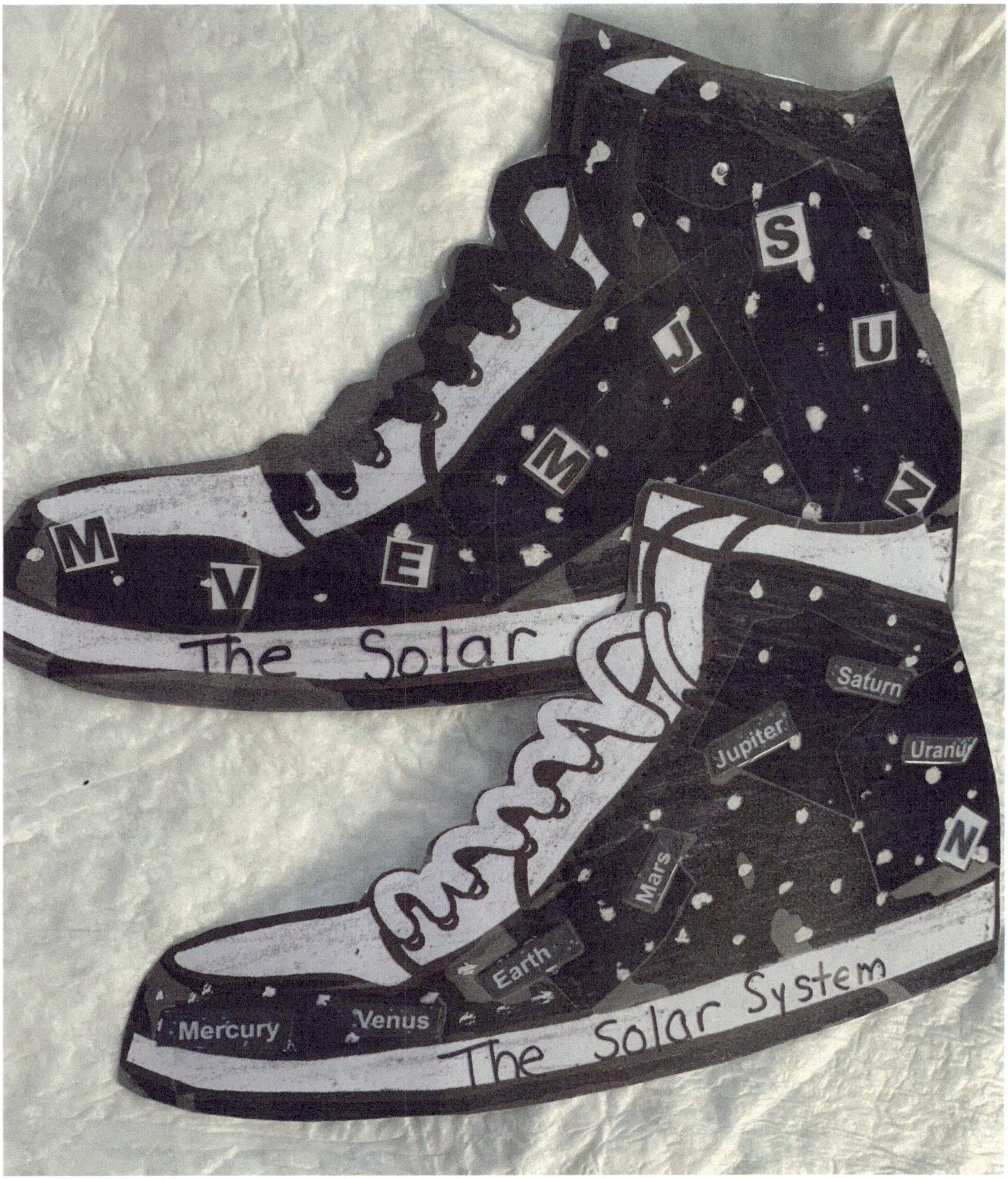
M
V
E
M
J
S
U
N
The Solar
Saturn
Jupiter
Uranu
N
Mars
Earth
Mercury
Venus
The Solar System

WE HAVE SO MANY DESIGNS
KEEP FLIPPING

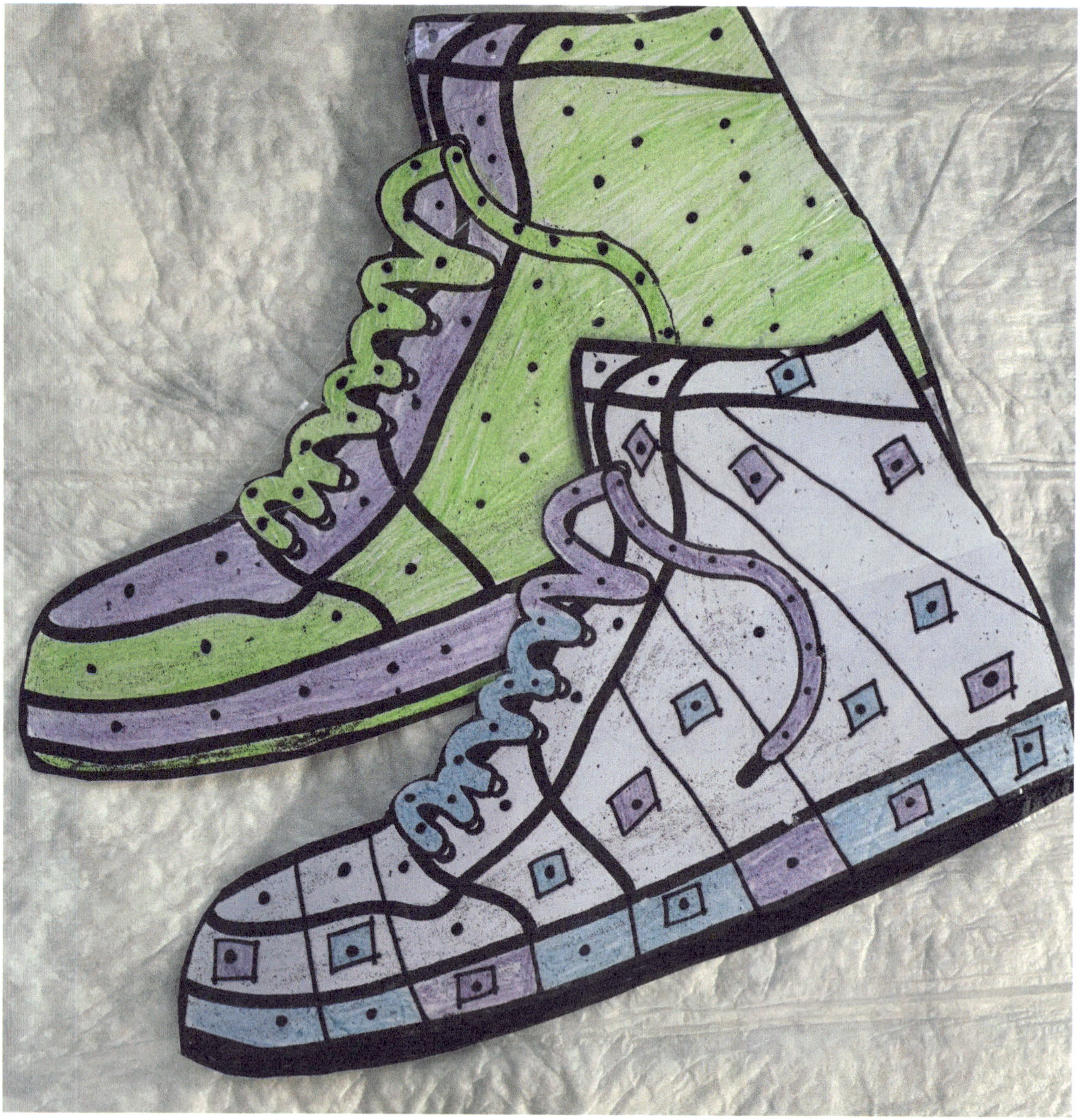

JUST BE CREATIVE

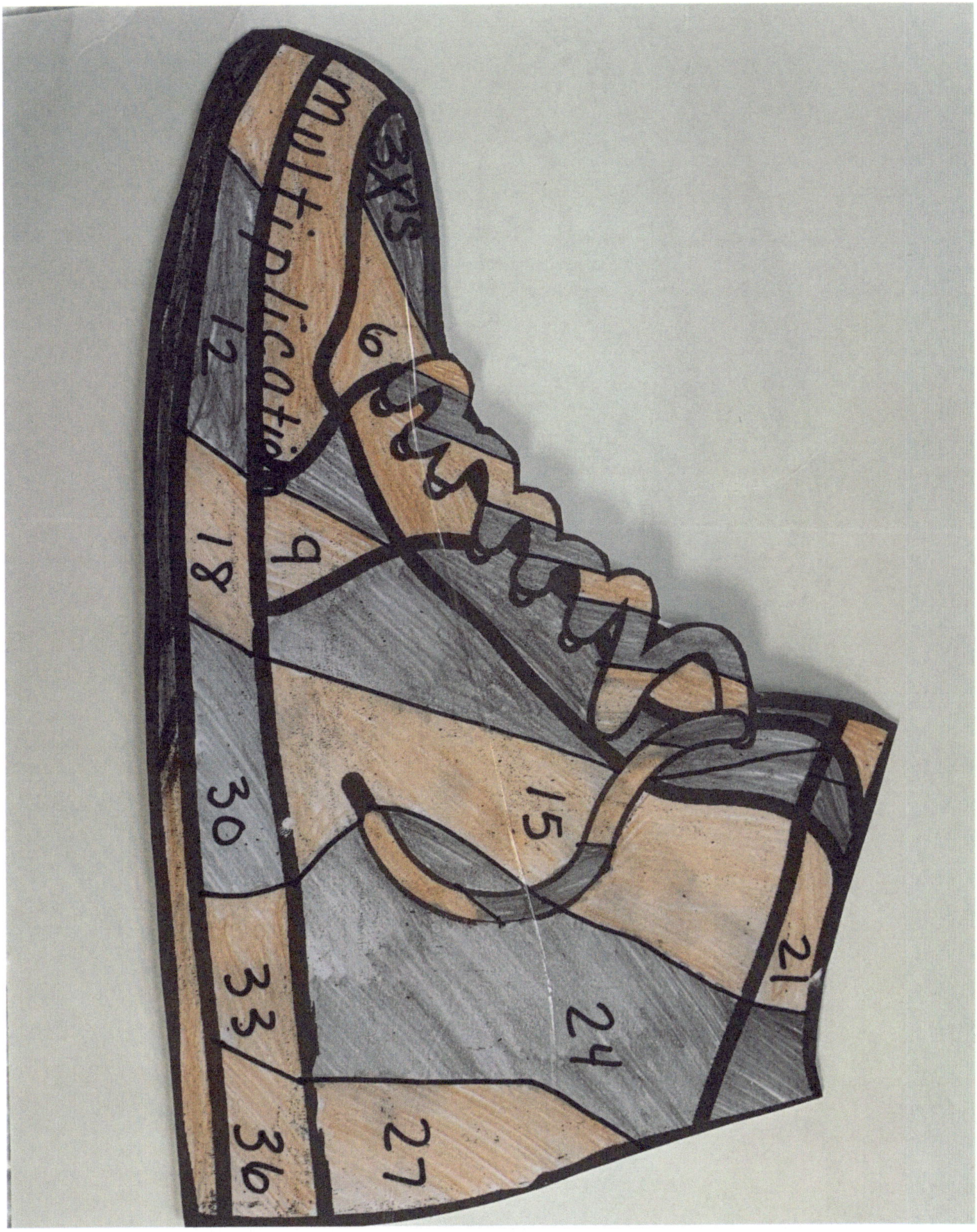
3X's
multiplication
6
9
12
15
18
21
24
27
30
33
36

# MATH IS FUN

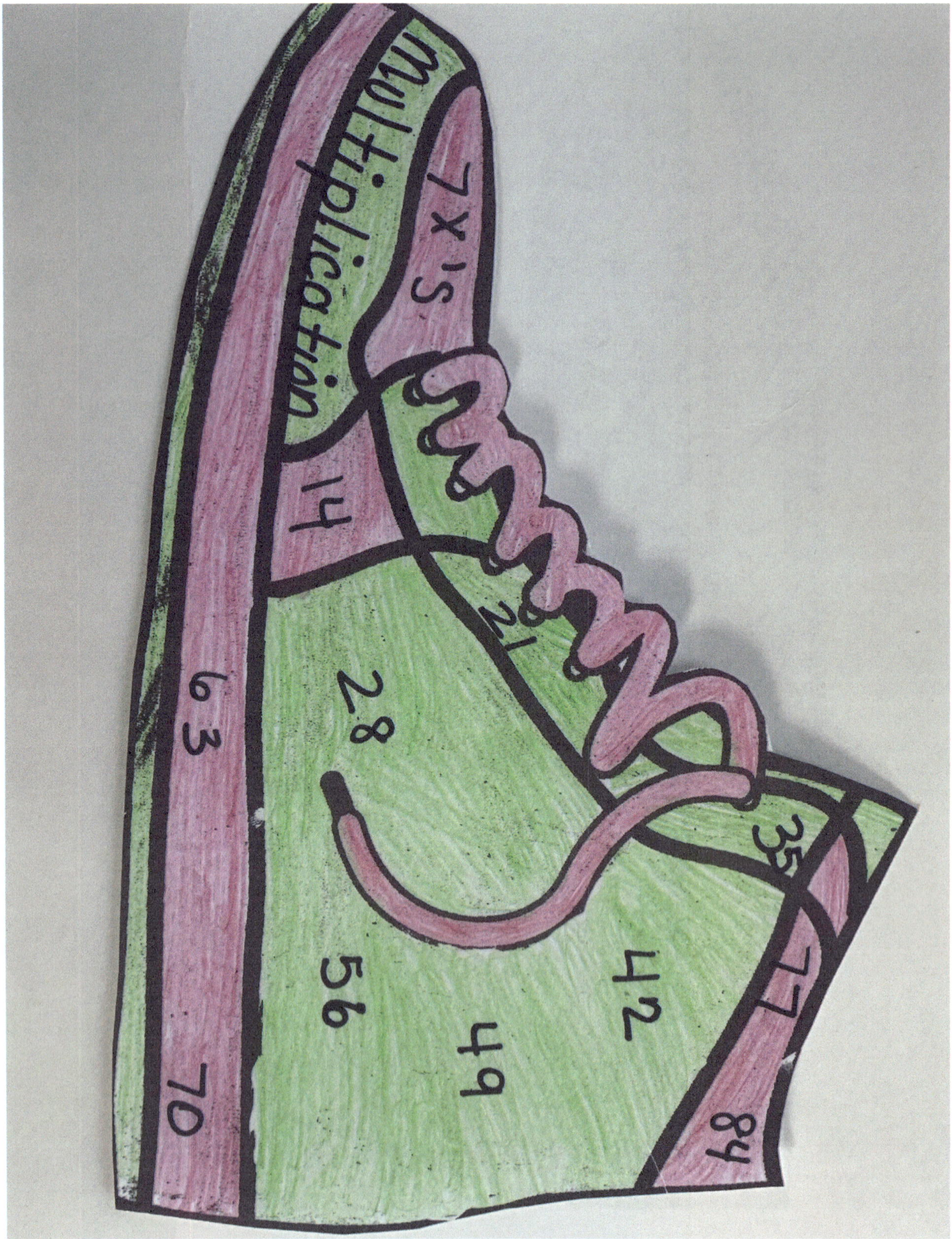
Multiplication
7x's
14
21
28
35
42
49
56
63
70
77
84

LEARNING IS FUN

Alphabet

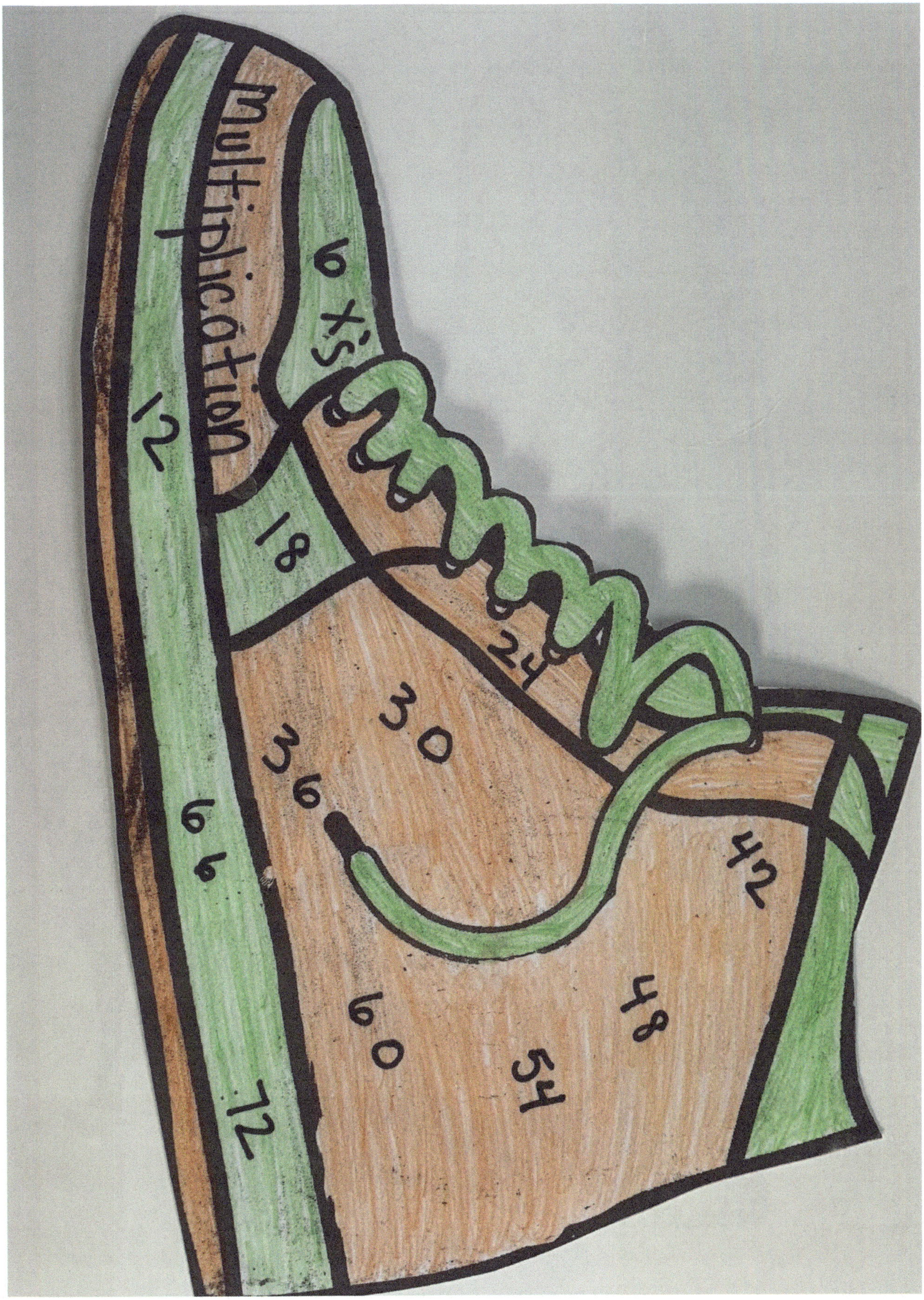
multiplication
6 x's
12
18
24
30
36
42
48
54
60
66
72

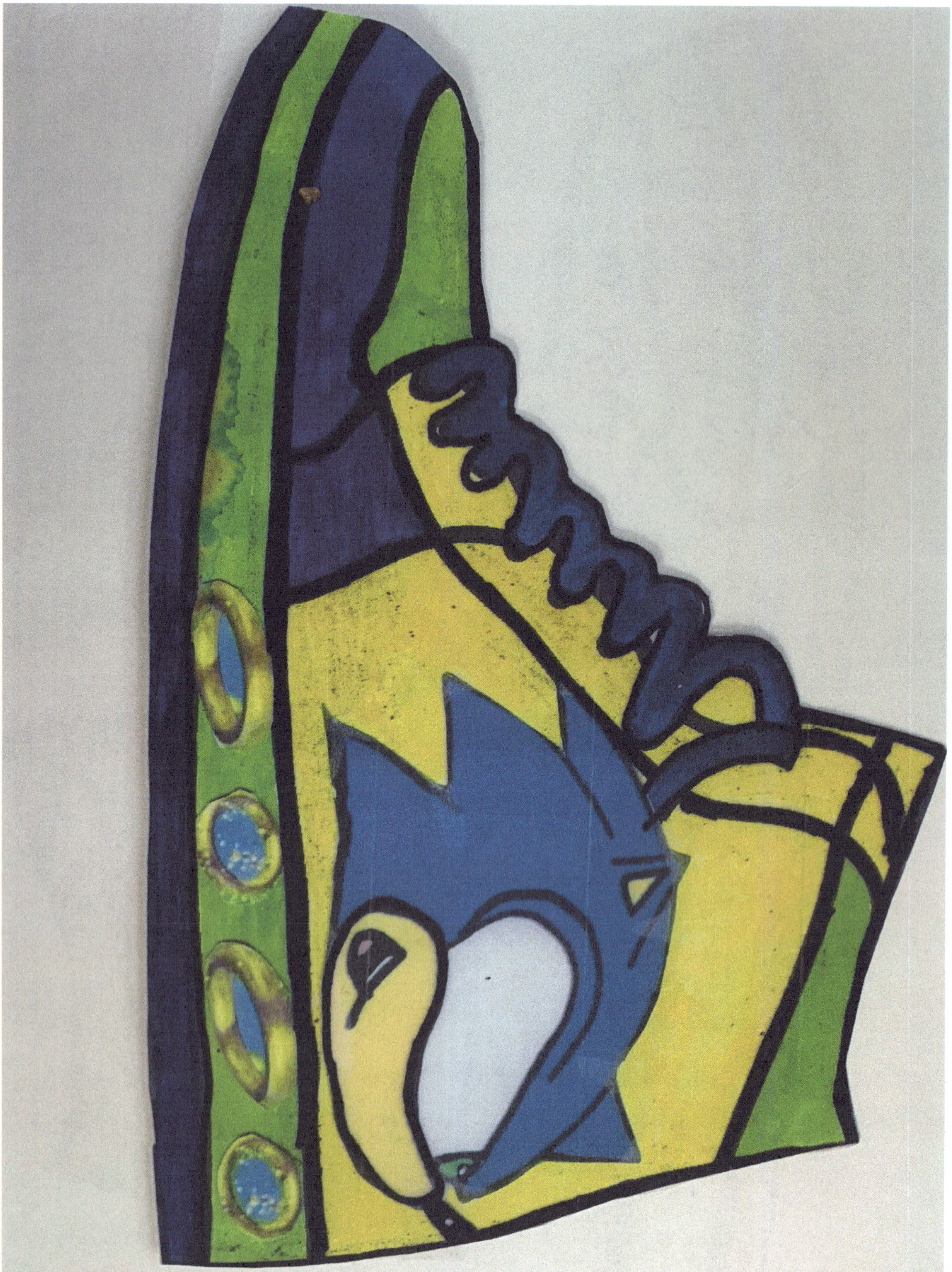

Alphabet

5
10
21
3
3X's
6
44
48
28
27
32
35
16
4 X's
multiplication
8
20
5X's
multiplication
15
42
48
54
24
6 X's
multiplication
30
35
77
84
18
42
12
21
7X's
multiplication
49
28
14
56
63
70

Blippi
Blippi

NIKE
NIKE

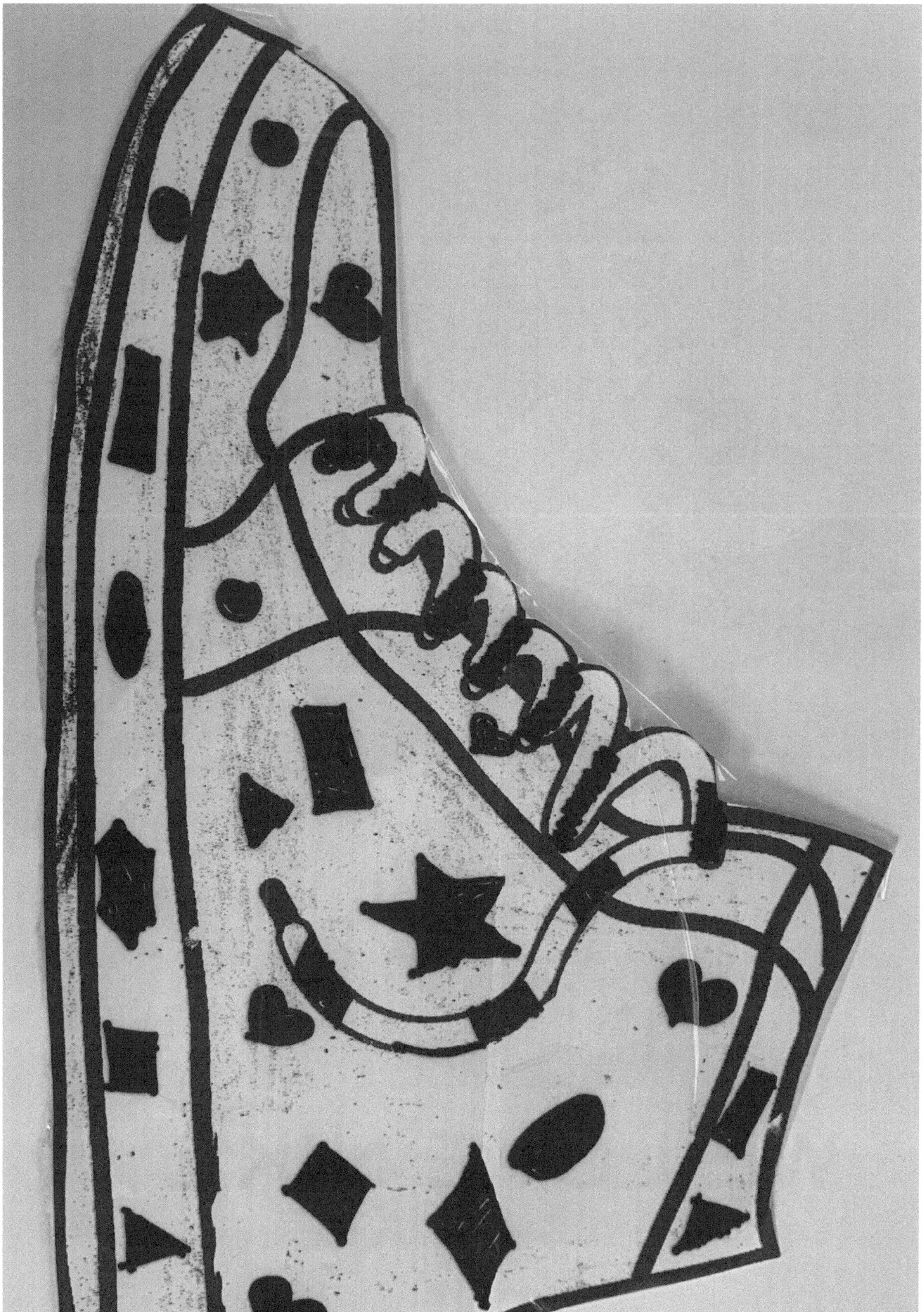

NIKE
NIKE
NIKE
NIKE

WE LOVE NIKE

M
M

MARIO

4 x's
multiplication
8
12
16
20
24
28
32
36
40
44
48

Calculator

# CAR RIDE IDEAS WITH BOOK RINGS

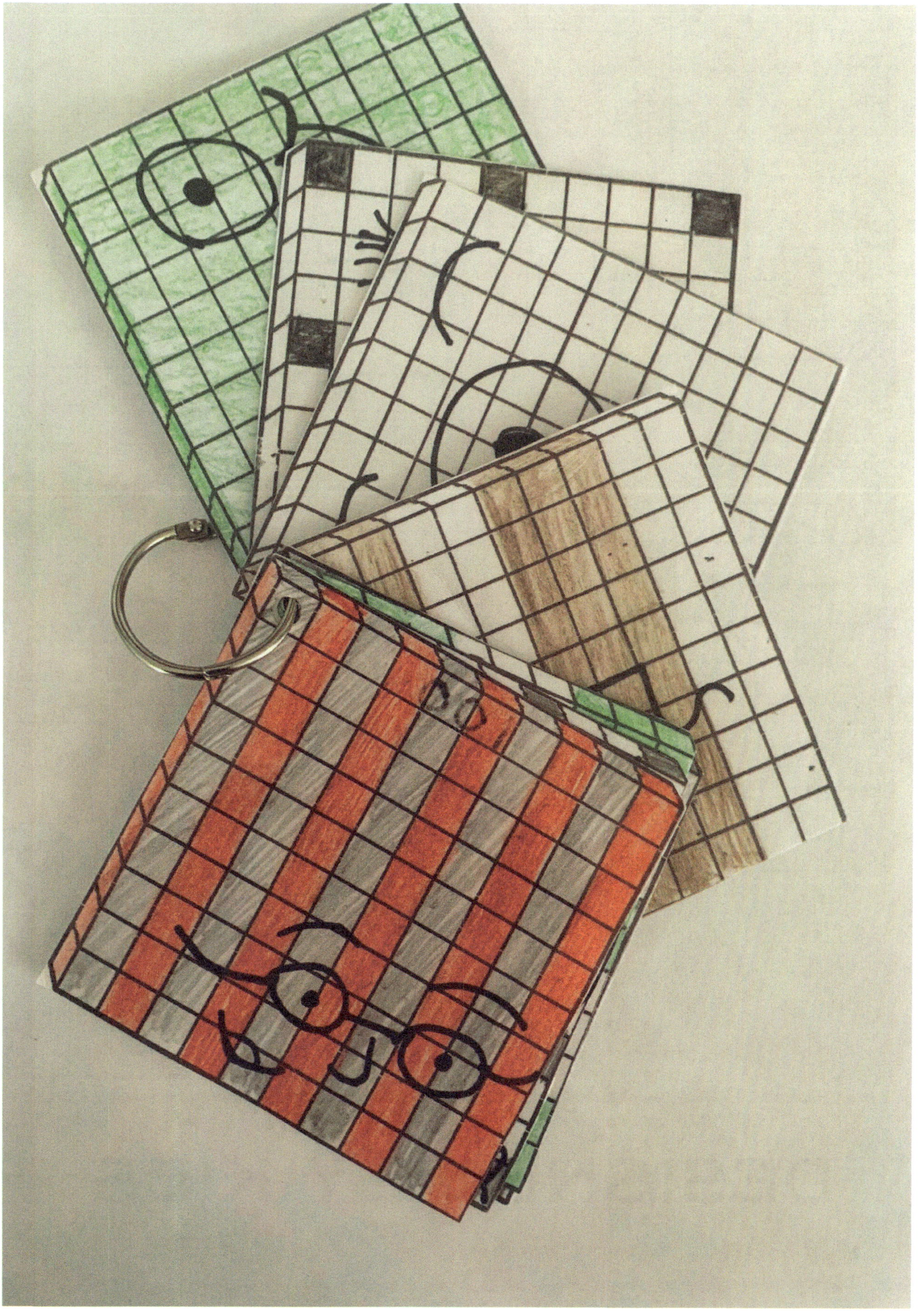

DESIGNED BY KIDS

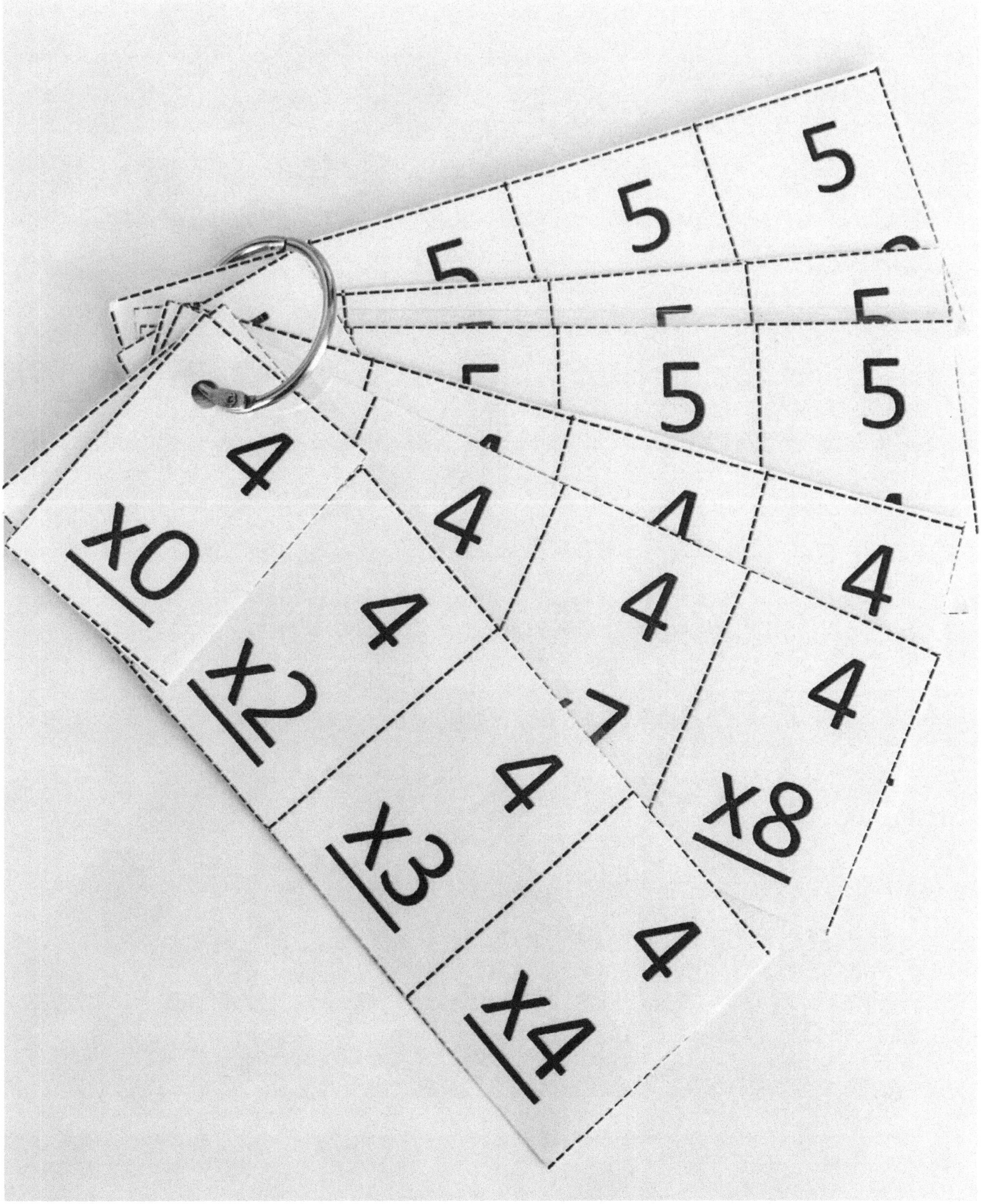
4
x0
4
x2
4
x3
4
x4
4
x8
5

KIDS CAN LEARN WITH
BOOK RINGS

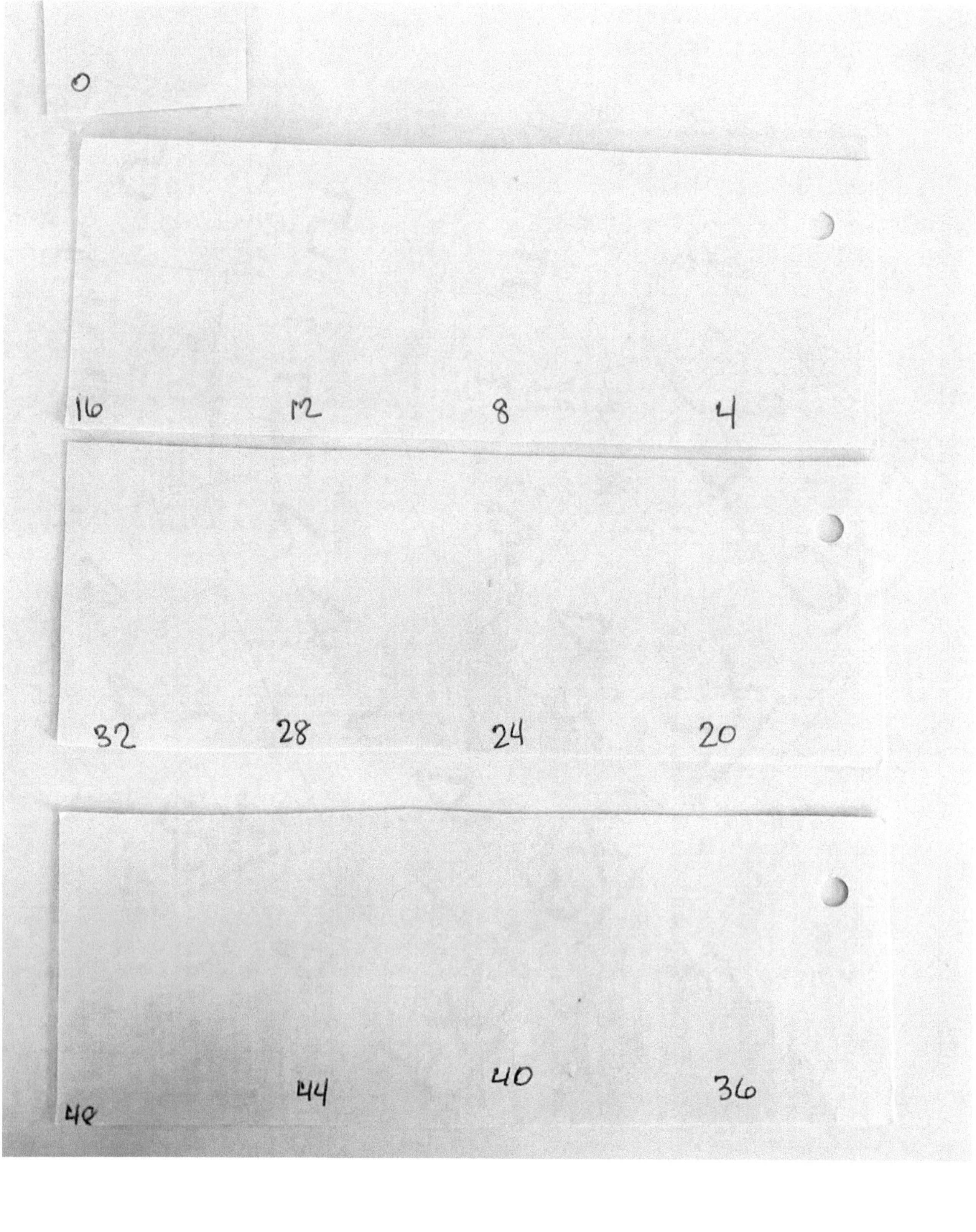
0
16
12
8
4
32
28
24
20
48
44
40
36

January
Sunday
Tuesday

January
Sunday
Monday
Tuesday
Wednesday
Thursday
Friday
Saturday

# FUN LEARNING

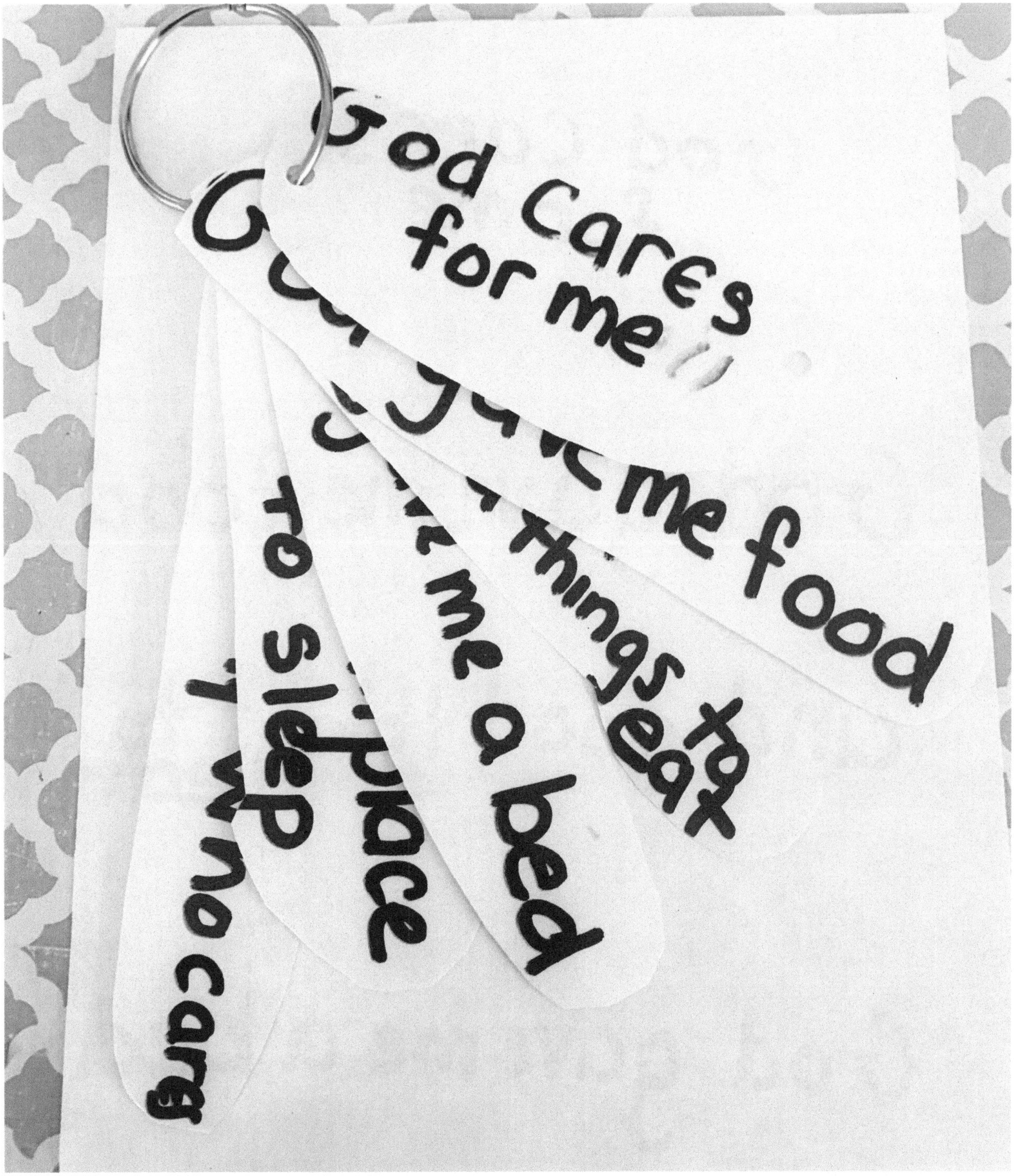
God cares for me
me food
things to eat
me a bed
place
to sleep

TRAVEL AND READ

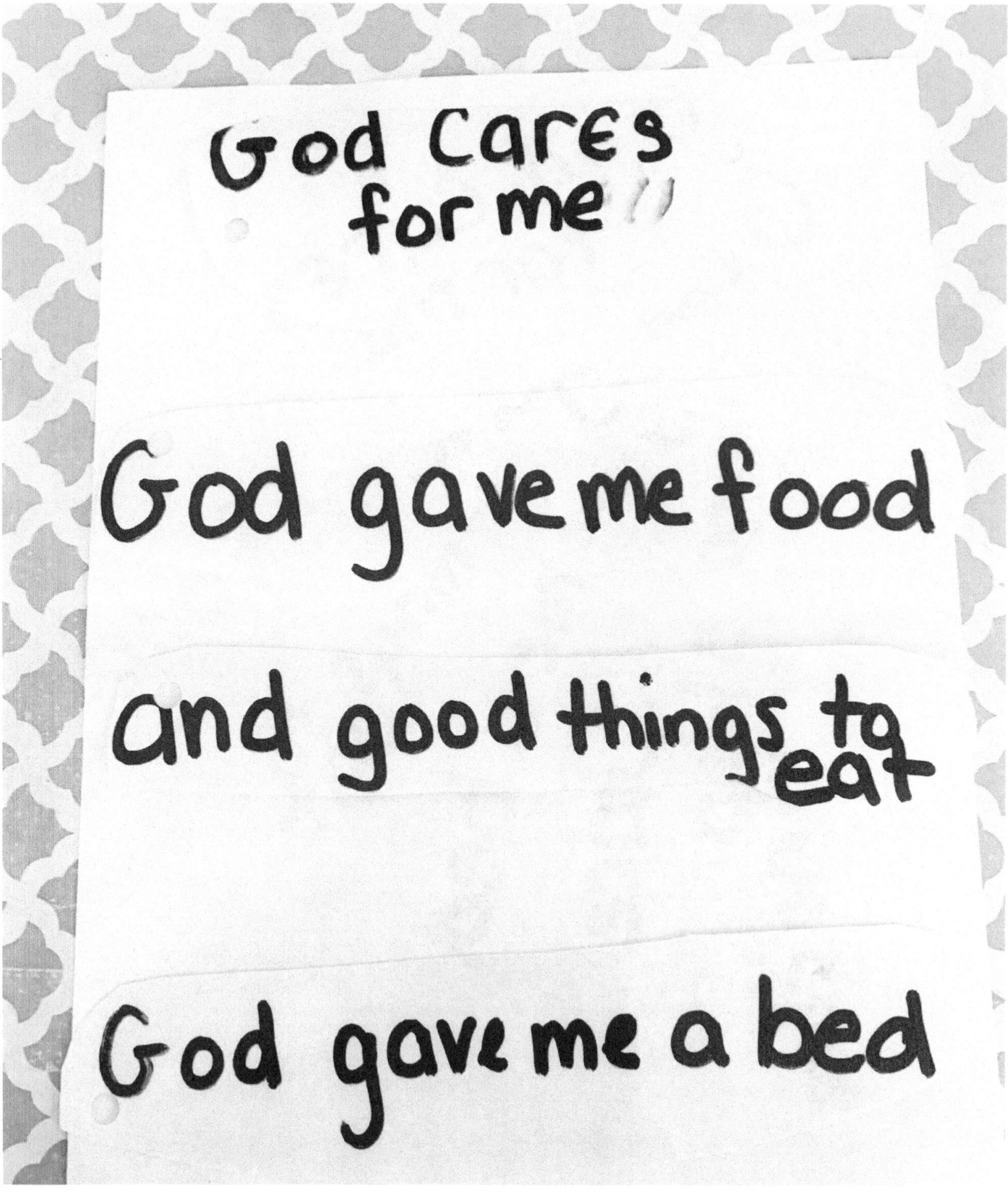
God Cares for me
God gave me food
and good things to eat
God gave me a bed

TURN YOUR KIDS BOOKS
INTO BOOK RINGS

and a warm place to sleep

God gave me a home

and a family who cares

100
FEDERAL RESERVE NOTE
COPY MONEY
10
5
MP
TWO DOLLARS
FEDERAL RESERVE NOTE
THE UNITED STATES OF AMERICA
ONE DOLLAR
WASHINGTON, D.C.
MONEY PRINTER
THIS NOTE IS NOT LEGAL TENDER

# KIDS CAN LEARN AND COUNT

FEDERAL RESERVE NOTE
THE UNITED STATES OF AMERICA
MONEY PRINTER
THIS NOTE IS NOT LEGAL TENDER
COPY MONEY
WASHINGTON, D.C.
COPY MONEY
SERIES 2009
ONE DOLLAR

TWO DOLLARS
FEDERAL RESERVE NOTE
TWO DOLLARS
MONEY PRINTER
THIS NOTE IS NOT LEGAL TENDER
COPY MONEY
WASHINGTON, D.C.
COPY MONEY
SERIES 2003 A
JEFFERSON
THE UNITED STATES OF AMERICA
TWO DOLLARS

FEDERAL
RESERVE NOTE
COPY MONEY
THE UNITED STATES OF AMERICA
MP
COPY MONEY
MONEY PRINTER
THIS NOTE IS NOT LEGAL TENDER
SERIES 2006
FIVE
LINCOLN
DOLLARS

10
FEDERAL
RESERVE NOTE
10
COPY MONEY
MP
THE UNITED STATES
OF AMERICA
MONEY PRINTER
THIS NOTE IS NOT LEGAL TENDER
SERIES
2004
A
Treasurer of the United States.
COPY MONEY
Secretary of the Treasury.
10
10
TEN
HAMILTON
DOLLARS

100
ONE HUNDRED DOLLARS
100
FEDERAL RESERVE NOTE
THE
UNITED STATES
OF AMERICA
COPY MONEY
MP
MONEY PRINTER
THIS NOTE IS NOT LEGAL TENDER
Secretary of the Treasury.
Treasurer of the United States.
COPY MONEY
SERIES
2009
100
100
FRANKLIN

# COOL WAYS TO TEACH KIDS ENGLISH AND SPANISH

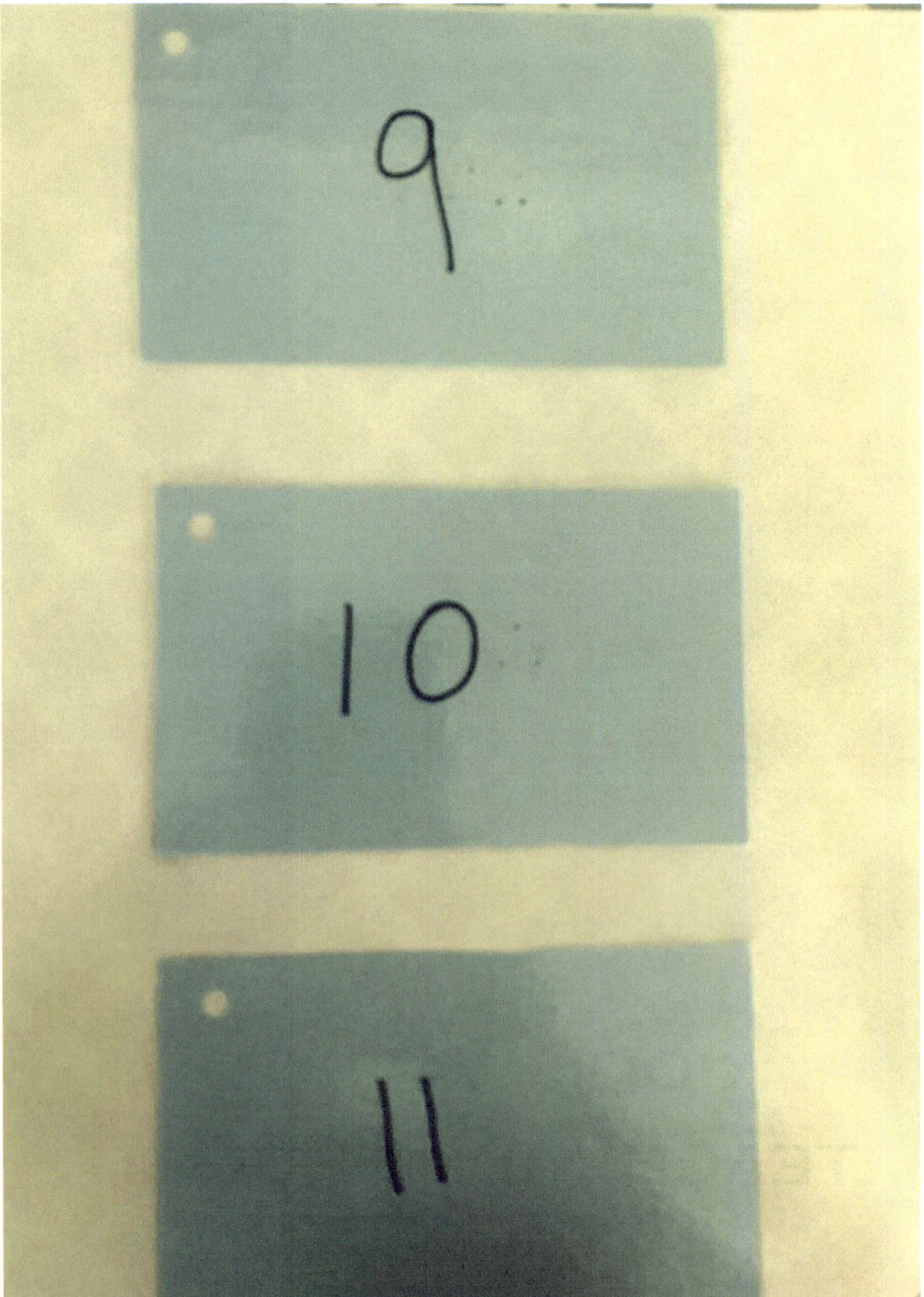
9
10
11

nueve
diez
once

SUN

SUN
MERCURY
VENUS
EARTH
MARS
JUPITER
SATURN
URANUS
NEPTUNE

Mercury
cury is the planet closest to our Sun.
a small, rocky planet much like our
n. It is covered with craters and has
nged very little from when it was first
ned. You can see Mercury with
oculars or with your eyes.
Venus is the
Because Venus
sometimes cal
Most of Venus'
rolling plains.
in the sky.
Earth is
71 % of
water.
water can ex
surface.
and unique of
also the most bea
Saturn is
and the sec
beautiful rings
some rocks an
composed of hy
does not have a
Sixty-two moons

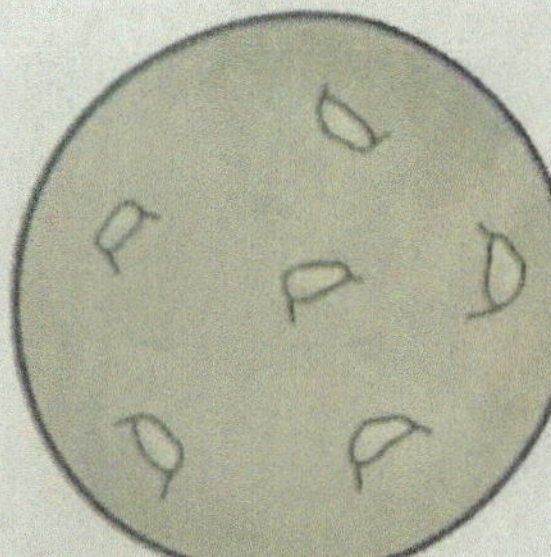

cury is the planet closest to our Sun.
: a small, rocky planet much like our
n. It is covered with craters and has
aged very little from when it was first
ned. You can see Mercury with
culars or with your eyes.

## Mercury

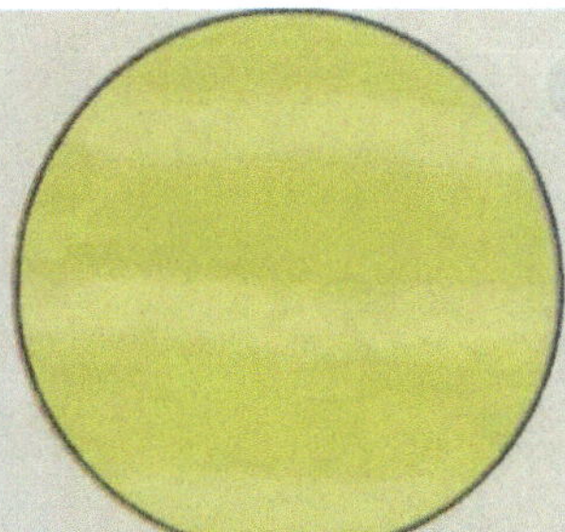

Venus is the second planet from the Sun. Because Venus is so similar to Earth, we sometimes call it Earth's "sister planet." Most of Venus' surface consists of gently rolling plains. It is the brightest "star" in the sky.

## Venus

Earth is the third planet from the Sun. 71 % of the Earth's surface is covered with water. Earth is the only planet on which water can exist in liquid form on the surface. Besides being the most interesting and unique of all the planets, our Earth is also the most beautiful.

## Earth

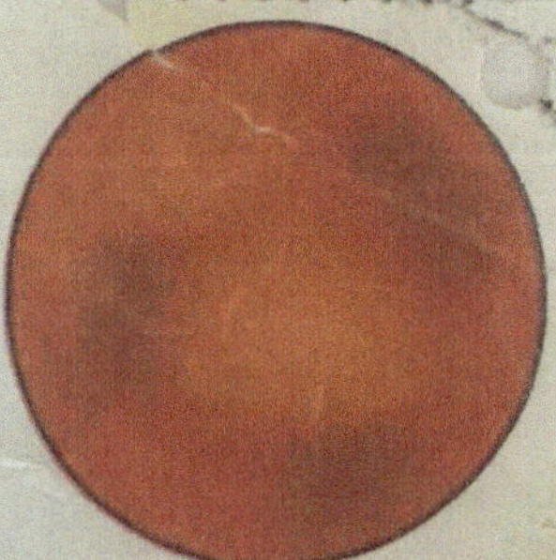

Mars is the fourth planet from the
It is often referred to as the Red Plan
Water erosion shows that it used to h
water. The southern part of Mar
mostly ancient, cratered highlands.
northern part consists mostly of plai

## Mars

ter is the fifth planet from the Sun
is the largest.
ter does not have a solid surface due
ts gaseous composition. The swirls
bands we see are the tops of clouds
in its atmosphere. Jupiter has faint
s like Saturn's, but much smaller.

## Jupiter

Saturn is the sixth planet from the Sun and the second largest. Saturn's nine beautiful rings are made of ice particles, some rocks and dust. Saturn is mainly composed of hydrogen and helium and does not have a solid surface.
Sixty-two moons orbit the planet.

## Saturn

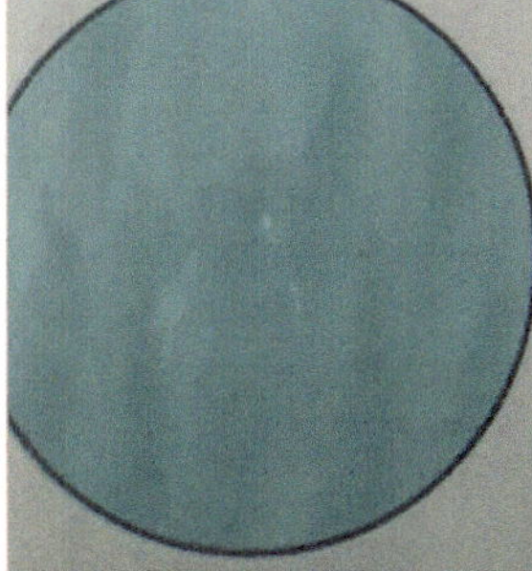

Uranus is the seventh planet from the Sun. Uranus' blue colour is the result of a gas called "methane". It has no solid surface. Like the other gas planets, Uranus has rings. Uranus' rings are very dark like Jupiter's rings.

## Uranus

Neptune is the eighth planet from the
Its' blue colour is the result of a gas ca
"methane". Neptune has rapid w
trapped in "bands" which are the fas
in the solar system, reaching 2000 l
hour! Neptune also has very dark
very faint rings.

## Neptune

toothpaste

eggs
dirty
sad
wide
smooth
sum
square
library
continent
sunflower
toothpaste
river

# CEREAL BOX PUZZLE IDEA

Kellogg's
APPLE JACKS
SWEETENED CEREAL WITH
APPLE & CINNAMON
CEREAL ENDULZADO CON MANZANA Y CANELA
ENLARGED TO SHOW TEXTURE
Agrandado para mostrar la textura
150 ALORIES
0.5g SAT FAT 3% DV
210mg SODIUM 9% DV
13g TOTAL SUGARS
ER 1 1/3 CUP SERVING

General Mills
FAMILY SIZE
18 OZ
Gluten Free
NO ARTIFICIAL FLAVORS
NO COLORS FROM ARTIFICIAL SOURCES
Multi Grain
Cheerios
WHOLE 28 grams GRAIN
per serving
Enlarged to Show Detail
100%
DAILY VALUE OF
9 VITAMINS & MINERALS
MAY reduce THE RISK OF HEART DISEASE*
AS PART OF A HEART HEALTHY DIET
150 CALORIES CALORÍAS
SAT FAT GRASA SAT
0% DV
150mg SODIUM SODIO
6% DV
8g TOTAL SUGARS AZÚCARES TOTALES
NET WT/PESO NETO
LB 2 OZ (18 OZ) (510g)
Endulzado

General Mills
MILY SIZE
Gluten F
WHOLE
Chos
GRAIN
per serving
DAIL
VAL
0%
AMINS
RALS
9 VITA
& MINER
MAY reduce
HEART
DISEASE
NET WT/PESO NETO
LB 2 OZ (18 OZ) (510g)
Sweetened Ce
Ligeramente
Lightly
Cere
Endulzado

General Mills
FA
AMILY SIZE
Gluten
Free
Mu
ulti Gra
ain
Chee
eri
os
WHOLE
GRAIN
per serving
DAIL
VAL
LUE
OF
9 VITA
AMINS
& MINE
RALS
10
0%
MAY reduce
HEART
DISEASE*
Sweetened Ce
real
eal Ligeramente
Endulzado
NET WT/PESO NETO
LB 2 OZ (18 OZ) (510g)
Lightly
Cere
150
CALORIES
CALORÍAS
150mg
SODIUM
SODIO
8g
TOTAL SUGARS
AZÚCARES TOTALES

# FUN IDEAS TO LEARN MATH

1
2
3
4
5
6
7
8

Match my number
90
01
37
79
01
65
79
90
65
37

5
5
5
5
4
x0
4
4
x2
4
x3
4
x4
4
4
4
x8

TODDLERS CAN LEARN

COPY MONEY
FEDERAL RESERVE NOTE
THE UNITED STATES OF AMERICA
WASHINGTON, D.C.
ONE DOLLAR
TWO DOLLARS

# FUN COUNTING

9

WE WROTE THE NUMBERS IN SPANISH ON THE BACK

1
2
3
4
5
6
7
8
9
10

WE ADDED THE EYES
FOR FUN LEARNING

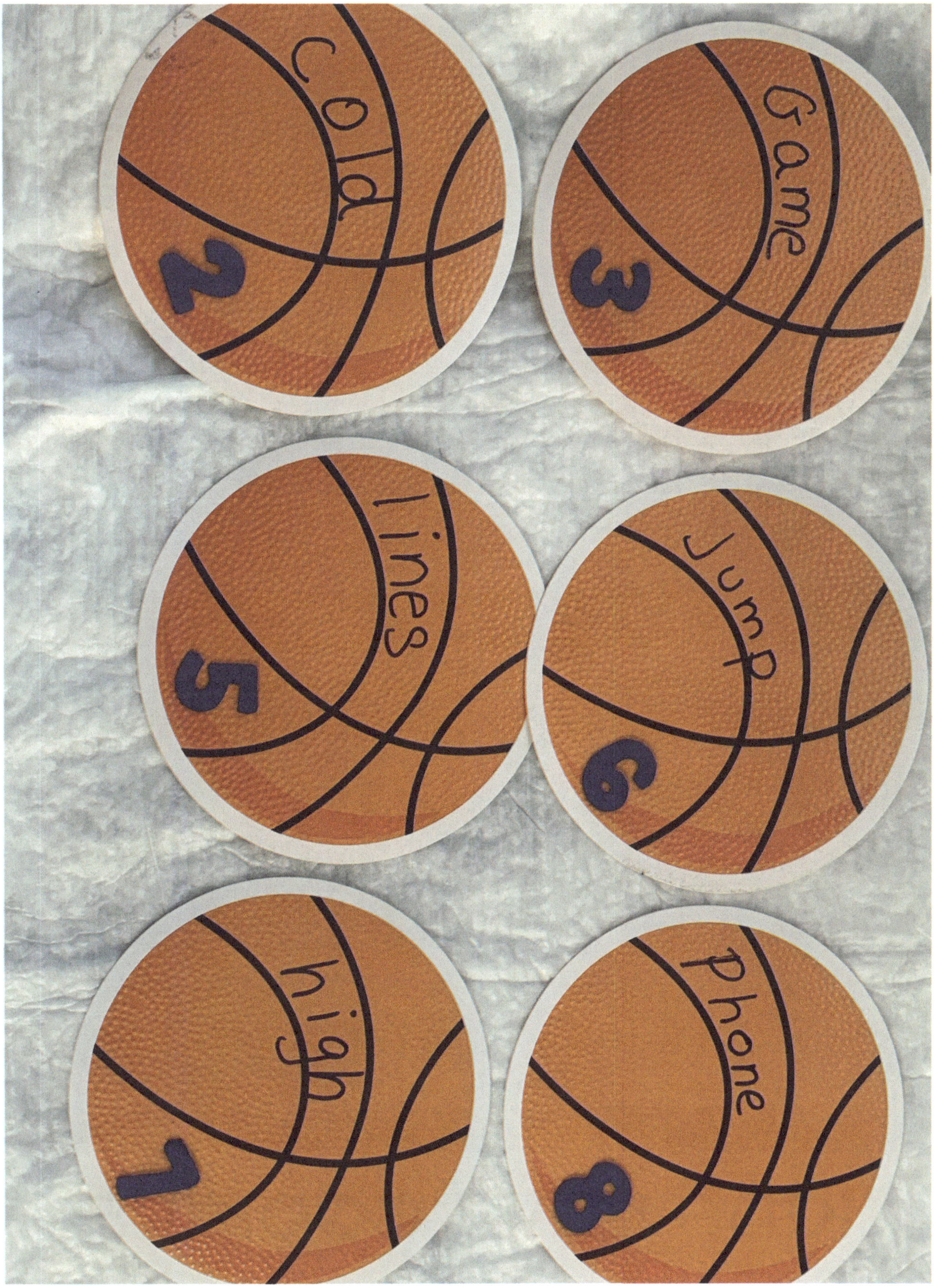
cold
2
Game
3
lines
5
jump
6
high
7
Phone
8

14
6
9

KIDS LOVE COOKIES

Find the letters/ numbers
S
7
3
5
N
0
2
8
G
m
9
X
F
U
a

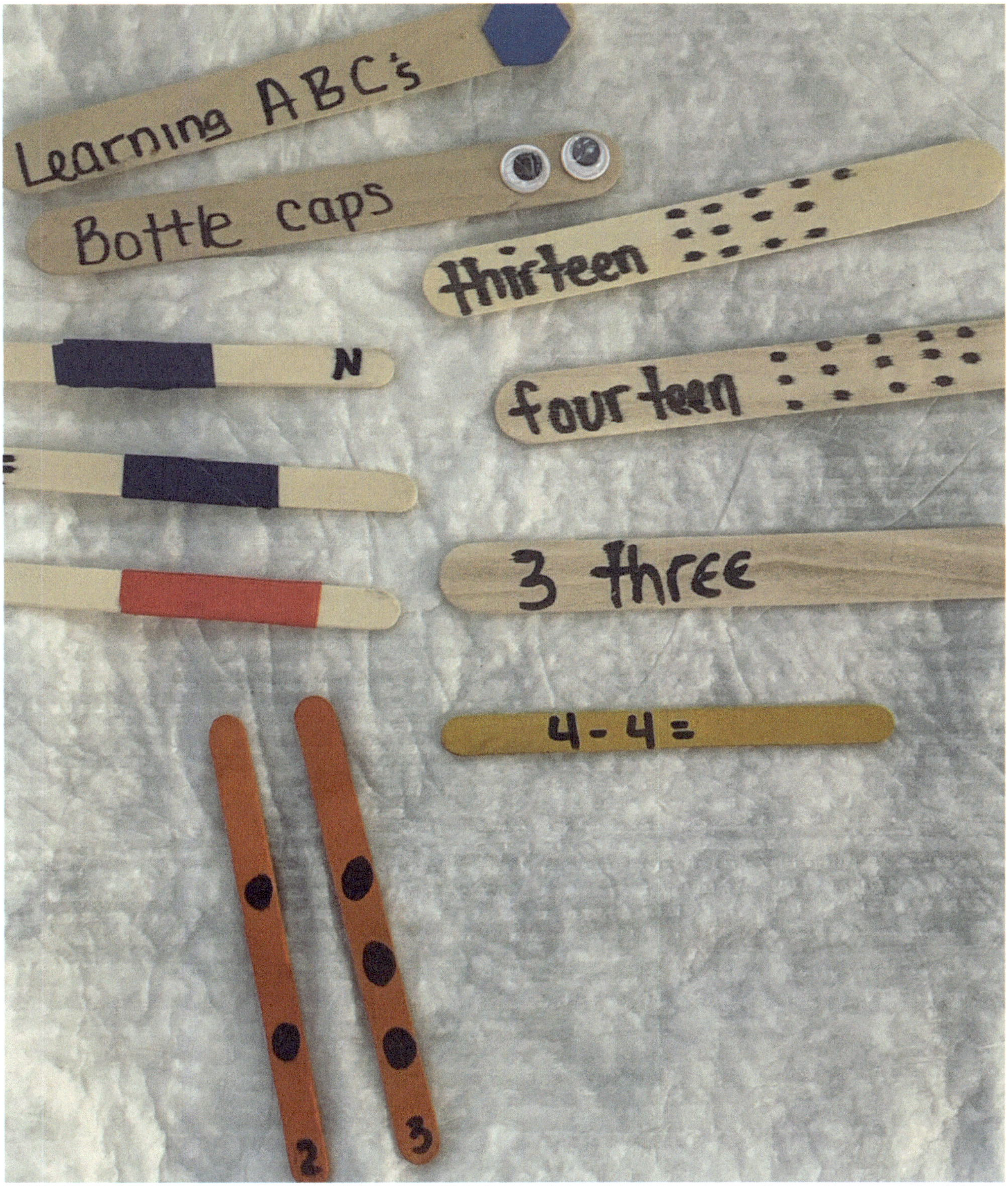
Learning ABC's
Bottle caps
thirteen
N
four teen
3 three
4 - 4 =
2
3

# FUN WAYS TO USE CRAFT STICKS

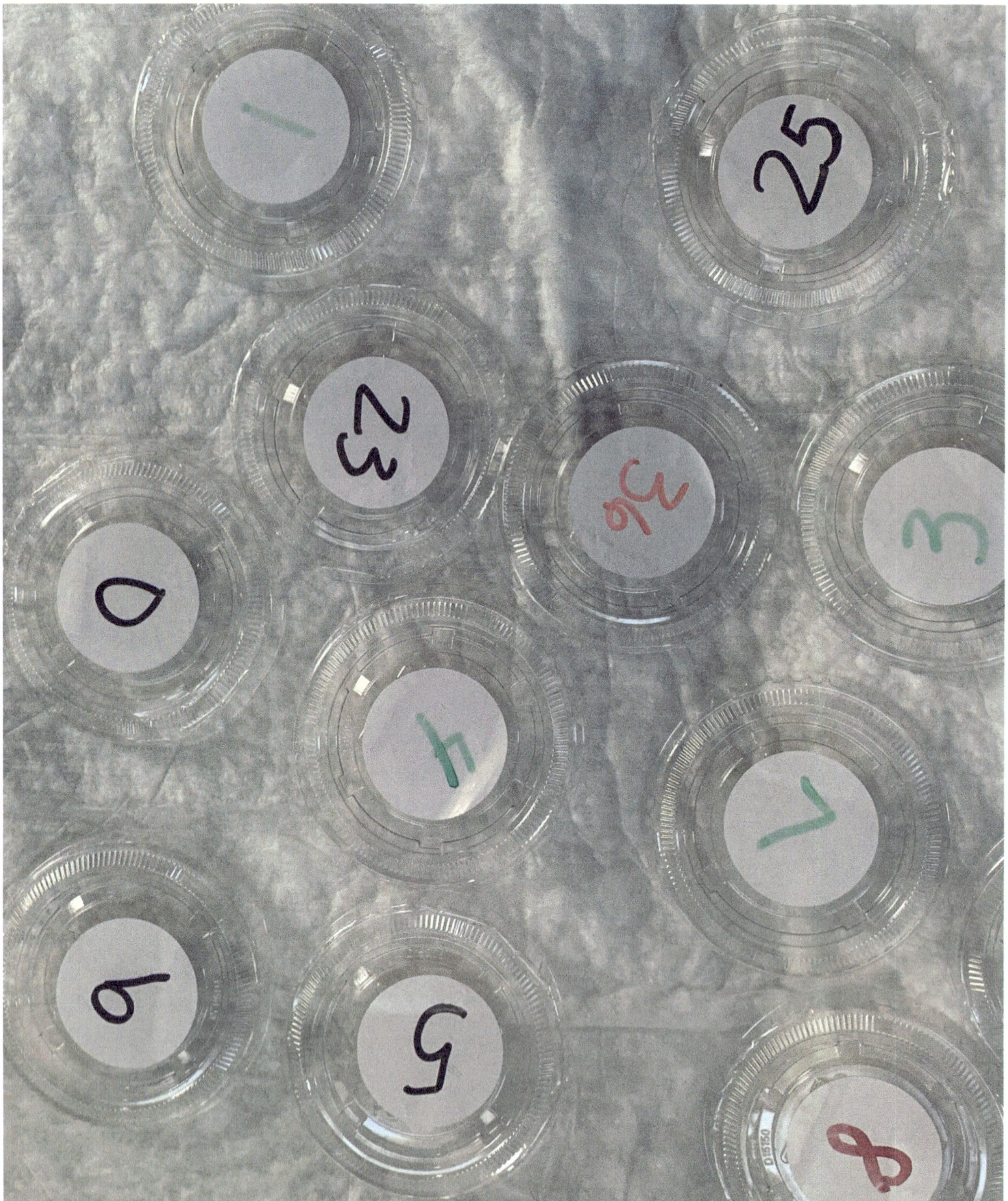

CONDIMENT
LIDS

Count my stripes
How many wheels

cinco
uno
seis
dos
nueve
tres
siete
diez
cuatro
ocho

# LEARN SPANISH

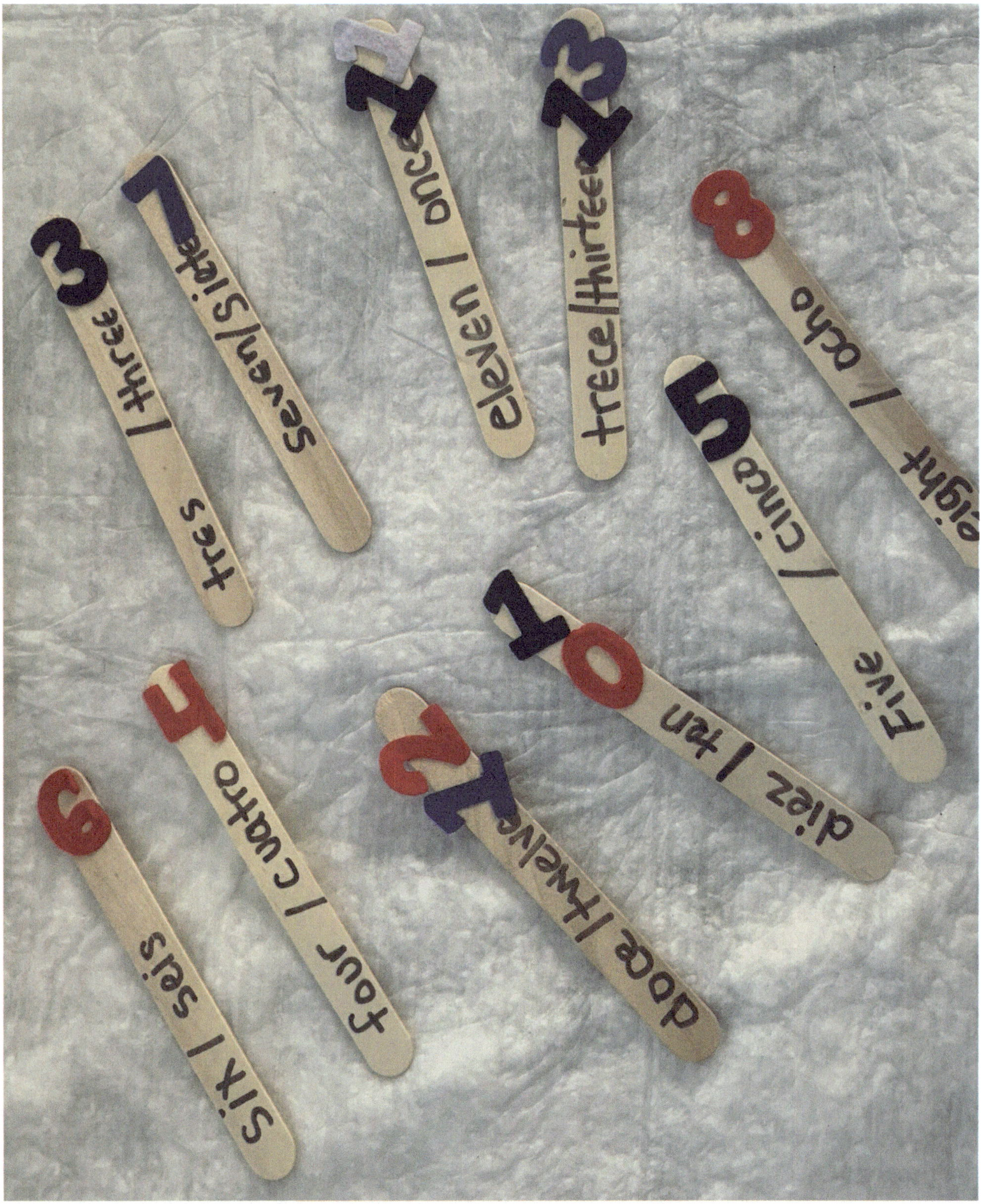

three / tres
seven/siete
eleven / once
eight / ocho
cinco / Five
diez / ten
doce / twelve
four / cuatro
six / seis


# LET'S LEARN SPANISH

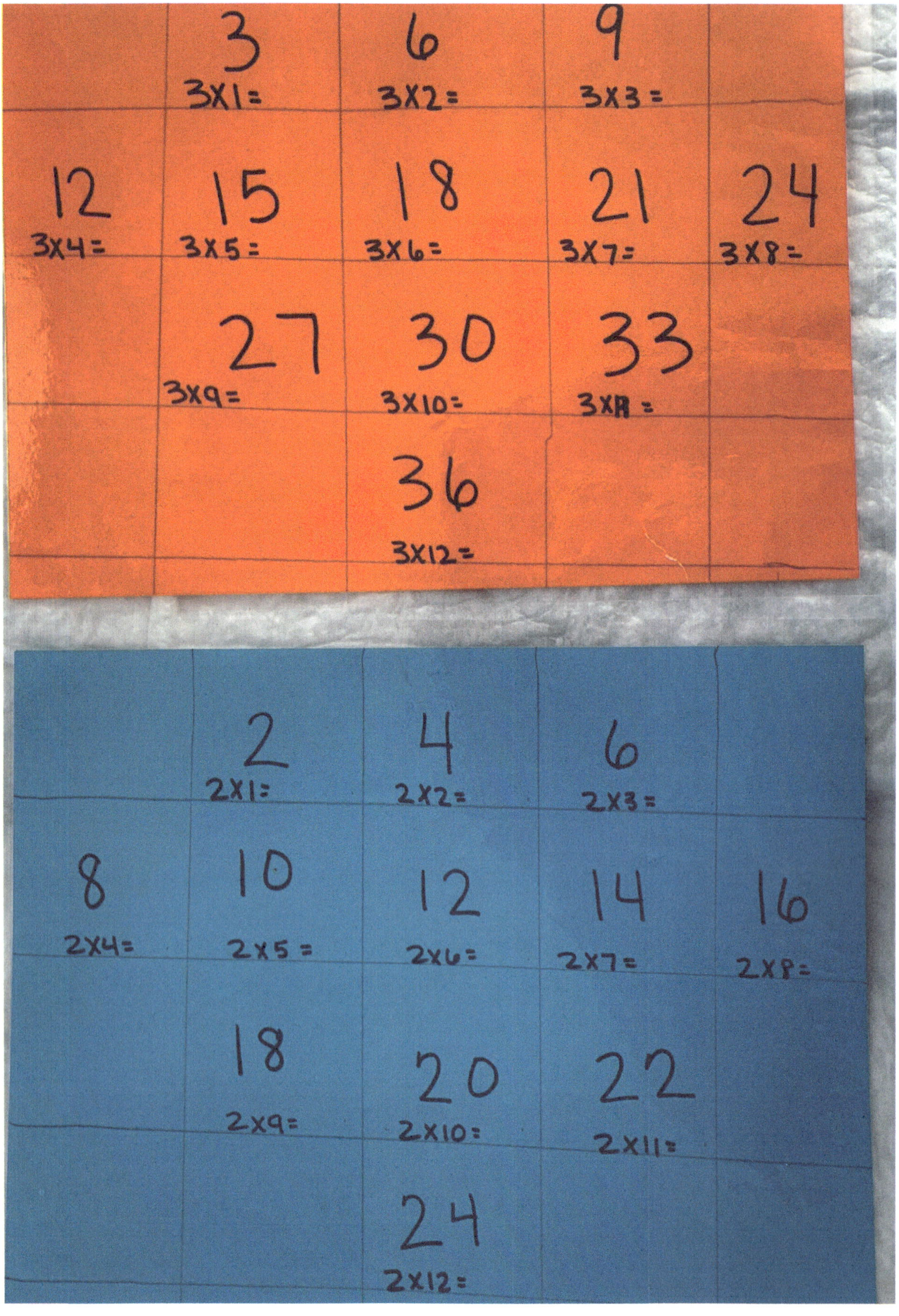
3
3X1=
6
3X2=
9
3X3=
12
3X4=
15
3X5=
18
3X6=
21
3X7=
24
3X8=
27
3X9=
30
3X10=
33
36
3X12=
2
2X1=
4
2X2=
6
2X3=
8
2X4=
10
2X5=
12
2X6=
14
2X7=
16
2X8=
18
2X9=
20
2X10=
22
2X11=
24
2X12=

1 uno
2 dos
3 Tres
4 cuatro
5 cinco
6 sieis

ENGLISH AND SPANISH

# NUMBERS 1-6

7 siete
8 ocho
9 nueve
10 diez

ENGLISH AND SPANISH
NUMBERS 7-10

# MULTIPLICATION

## WATER BOTTLE WHEEL

# MULTIPLICATION WATER BOTTLE WHEEL

## STEP 1

GET A PAIR OF SCISSORS

## STEP 2

CUT THE TOP AND THE BOTTOM OFF

## STEP 3

ADD YOUR NUMBERS AROUND THE BOTTLE

## STEP 4

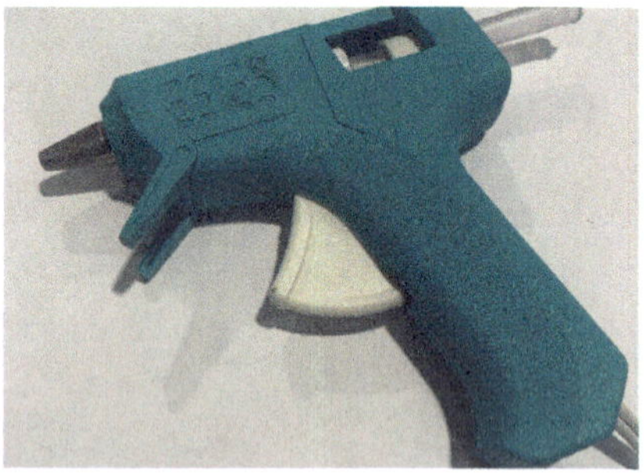

HOT GLUE THE INSIDE OF THE BOTTLE ON BOTH SIDES

## STEP 5

USE YOUR CRAFT STICKS TO PUT ON THE INSIDE OF THE BOTTLE

1 2 3
4 5 6
7 8 9
0
i phone
2 3
4 6
7 8
Hello

# CELL PHONES

# FUN WAYS KIDS CAN LEARN WORDS

paper
chalk
eraser
globe
coat
backpack
flag
chalkboard
phone
desk
clock
pencil
easel
computer
door
scissors
calculator
books
window
pencil sharpener
crayons
paintbrush
paint
wastebasket
pen
lunch box
ruler

because
funny
and
gave
fly
but
her
is
cow
sleep
may

# LAMINATED INDEX CARD

Read and write

EAT

FIX

GIRL

Monday
Tuesday
Wednesday
Thursday
Friday
Saturday
Sunday

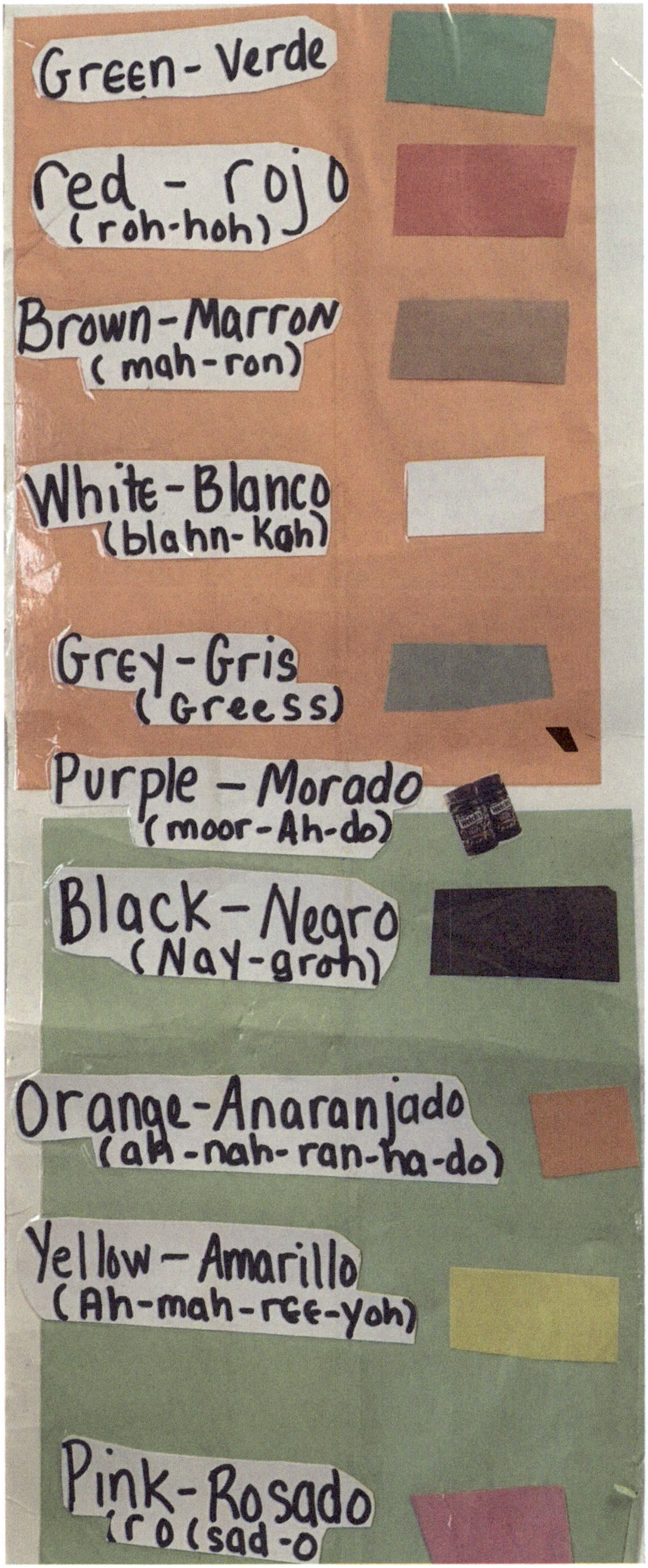
Green- Verde
red - rojo
(roh-hoh)
Brown-Marron
(mah-ron)
White-Blanco
(blahn-Koh)
Grey-Gris
(Greess)
Purple - Morado
(moor-Ah-do)
Black-Negro
(Nay-groh)
Orange-Anaranjado
(ah-nah-ran-ha-do)
Yellow-Amarillo
(Ah-mah-ree-yoh)
Pink-Rosado

KIDS CAN
**LEARN**
ENGLISH
AND
SPANISH
COLORS

heart yellow
blue triangle
star blue
triangle yellow
pink heart
circle red
circle yellow
diamond yellow
circle green

invited
coming
taping
dropping
loved
changing
saving
Swimming
Stared
planned

eggs
dirty
sad
wide
smooth
sum
square
library
continent
sunflower
toothpaste
river

KIDS CAN LEARN WHILE
RIDING IN THE CAR

Lunes
(Monday)
Martes
(Tuesday)
miërcoles
(wednesday)
Jueves
(Thursday)
Viernes
(Friday)
Sábado
(Saturday)
Domingo
(Sunday)

# ARTS AND CRAFTS IDEAS

What do you see?

January
STICK
BED

Patterns

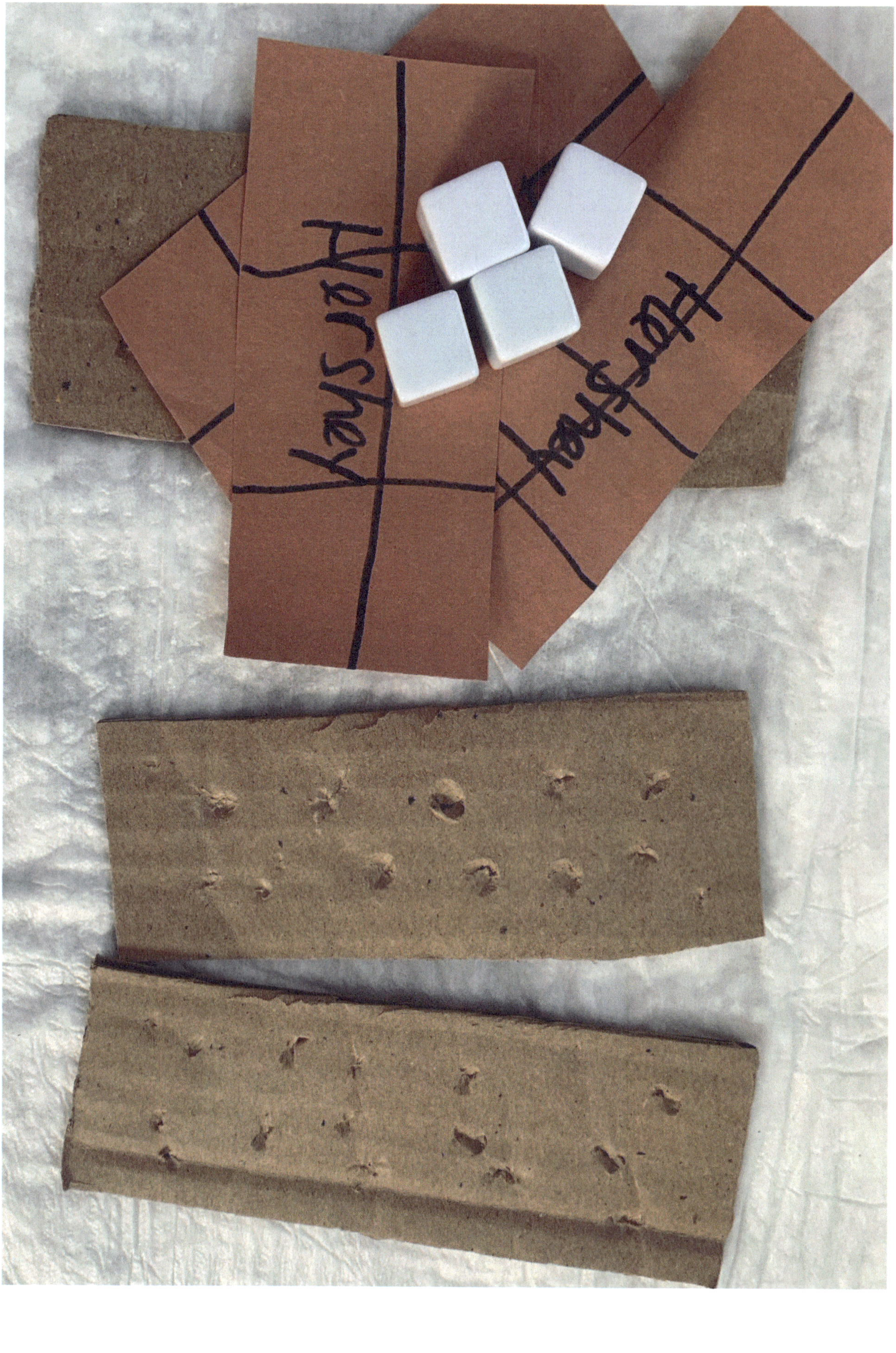
Hershey
Hershey

5
3
4
2

happy

FEELINGS MIRROR
WE LAMINATED A PAPER PLATE
KIDS CAN LOOK THROUGH AND
EXPLAIN
HOW THEY ARE FEELING

red
gripped
joking
giving
every
meterologist
tasted
after
round
again

Match the
Colors

FUN

THANK YOU FOR YOUR PURCHASE

WE HOPE THAT YOU FOUND SOME NEW IDEAS THAT WILL HELP YOU ON YOUR HOME SCHOOL JOURNEY

THIS JOURNEY CAN BE TOUGH SOME TIMES BUT YOU GOT THIS

.

WE HOPE YOU ENJOYED SOME NEW IDEAS THAT WILL HELP YOU FIND YOUR DAYS EASIER

I TAUGHT MY TODDLERS MULTIPLICATION WITH WATER BOTTLES AND STICKERS AND SO CAN YOU

Made in the USA
Columbia, SC
07 August 2023

21138722R00059